AF885216

APPOINTMENTS & MEETINGS

Where Minds Meet Intentions Align and Actions Follow

Presence. Alignment. Action.

ISBN 978-1-971308-04-3

Appointments & Meetings

Where Minds Meet, Intentions Align, and Actions Follow is more than a meeting notes book—it is a space of presence, precision, and purposeful movement.

In a world filled with conversations that scatter attention and meetings that end without clarity, this book serves as a quiet anchor. It invites you to slow the moment just enough to listen deeply, think clearly, and capture what truly matters. Here, dialogue becomes direction, insight becomes agreement, and intention becomes action.

Designed for leaders, creators, facilitators, and teams who value meaning as much as momentum, this meetings and notes book transforms the way conversations are held and completed. Each page offers a structured yet spacious framework to record key insights, decisions, action steps, and commitments—ensuring that nothing essential is lost and nothing important remains unfinished.

At its heart, this book honors time as sacred and attention as powerful. When minds meet with presence and intentions align with truth, action follows naturally and with integrity. This is where clarity replaces confusion, responsibility replaces assumption, and progress replaces repetition.

Whether used in executive meetings, collaborative sessions, coaching conversations, or personal planning, this book becomes a trusted companion—holding the intelligence of the room and guiding it toward meaningful outcomes. It supports focused dialogue, conscious leadership, and the completion of what has been agreed upon.

This is not about capturing every word. It is about capturing the right ones—the decisions that shape direction, the commitments that move vision forward, and the next steps that transform conversation into impact.

APPOINTMENTS
&
MEETINGS

Where Minds Meet Intentions Align and Actions Follow

Appointments & Meetings
by ThinkVirtues®
Find more Planners, Workbooks, and
a Master Collection of Virtues at ThinkVirtues.com

TOPIC OF MEETING	DAY / DATE

NOTES

ACTION ITEMS	DUE

Thoughts become words. Words become action. Actions become character. Character becomes destiny.

TOPIC OF MEETING	DAY / DATE

NOTES

ACTION ITEMS	DUE

Thoughts become words. Words become action. Actions become character. Character becomes destiny.

TOPIC OF MEETING	DAY / DATE

NOTES

ACTION ITEMS	DUE

Thoughts become words. Words become action. Actions become character. Character becomes destiny.

TOPIC OF MEETING	DAY / DATE

NOTES

ACTION ITEMS	DUE

Thoughts become words. Words become action. Actions become character. Character becomes destiny.

TOPIC OF MEETING	DAY / DATE

NOTES

ACTION ITEMS	DUE

Thoughts become words. Words become action. Actions become character. Character becomes destiny.

TOPIC OF MEETING	DAY / DATE

NOTES

ACTION ITEMS	DUE

Thoughts become words. Words become action. Actions become character. Character becomes destiny.

TOPIC OF MEETING	DAY / DATE

NOTES

ACTION ITEMS	DUE

Thoughts become words. Words become action. Actions become character. Character becomes destiny.

TOPIC OF MEETING	DAY / DATE

NOTES

ACTION ITEMS	DUE

Thoughts become words. Words become action. Actions become character. Character becomes destiny.

TOPIC OF MEETING	DAY / DATE

NOTES

ACTION ITEMS	DUE

Thoughts become words. Words become action. Actions become character. Character becomes destiny.

TOPIC OF MEETING	DAY / DATE

NOTES

ACTION ITEMS	DUE

Thoughts become words. Words become action. Actions become character. Character becomes destiny.

TOPIC OF MEETING	DAY / DATE

NOTES

ACTION ITEMS	DUE

Thoughts become words. Words become action. Actions become character. Character becomes destiny.

TOPIC OF MEETING	DAY / DATE

NOTES

ACTION ITEMS	DUE

Thoughts become words. Words become action. Actions become character. Character becomes destiny.

TOPIC OF MEETING	DAY / DATE

NOTES

ACTION ITEMS	DUE

Thoughts become words. Words become action. Actions become character. Character becomes destiny.

TOPIC OF MEETING	DAY / DATE

NOTES

ACTION ITEMS	DUE

Thoughts become words. Words become action. Actions become character. Character becomes destiny.

TOPIC OF MEETING	DAY / DATE

NOTES

ACTION ITEMS	DUE

Thoughts become words. Words become action. Actions become character. Character becomes destiny.

TOPIC OF MEETING	DAY / DATE

NOTES

ACTION ITEMS	DUE

Thoughts become words. Words become action. Actions become character. Character becomes destiny.

TOPIC OF MEETING	DAY / DATE

NOTES

ACTION ITEMS	DUE

Thoughts become words. Words become action. Actions become character. Character becomes destiny.

TOPIC OF MEETING	DAY / DATE

NOTES

ACTION ITEMS	DUE

Thoughts become words. Words become action. Actions become character. Character becomes destiny.

TOPIC OF MEETING	DAY / DATE

NOTES

ACTION ITEMS	DUE

Thoughts become words. Words become action. Actions become character. Character becomes destiny.

TOPIC OF MEETING	DAY / DATE

NOTES

ACTION ITEMS	DUE

Thoughts become words. Words become action. Actions become character. Character becomes destiny.

TOPIC OF MEETING	DAY / DATE

NOTES

ACTION ITEMS	DUE

Thoughts become words. Words become action. Actions become character. Character becomes destiny.

TOPIC OF MEETING	DAY / DATE

NOTES

ACTION ITEMS	DUE

Thoughts become words. Words become action. Actions become character. Character becomes destiny.

TOPIC OF MEETING	DAY / DATE

NOTES

ACTION ITEMS	DUE

Thoughts become words. Words become action. Actions become character. Character becomes destiny.

TOPIC OF MEETING	DAY / DATE

NOTES

ACTION ITEMS	DUE

Thoughts become words. Words become action. Actions become character. Character becomes destiny.

TOPIC OF MEETING	DAY / DATE

NOTES

ACTION ITEMS	DUE

Thoughts become words. Words become action. Actions become character. Character becomes destiny.

TOPIC OF MEETING	DAY / DATE

NOTES

ACTION ITEMS	DUE

Thoughts become words. Words become action. Actions become character. Character becomes destiny.

TOPIC OF MEETING	DAY / DATE

NOTES

ACTION ITEMS	DUE

Thoughts become words. Words become action. Actions become character. Character becomes destiny.

TOPIC OF MEETING	DAY / DATE

NOTES

ACTION ITEMS	DUE

Thoughts become words. Words become action. Actions become character. Character becomes destiny.

TOPIC OF MEETING	DAY / DATE

NOTES

ACTION ITEMS	DUE

Thoughts become words. Words become action. Actions become character. Character becomes destiny.

TOPIC OF MEETING	DAY / DATE

NOTES

ACTION ITEMS	DUE

Thoughts become words. Words become action. Actions become character. Character becomes destiny.

TOPIC OF MEETING	DAY / DATE

NOTES

ACTION ITEMS	DUE

Thoughts become words. Words become action. Actions become character. Character becomes destiny.

TOPIC OF MEETING	DAY / DATE

NOTES

ACTION ITEMS	DUE

Thoughts become words. Words become action. Actions become character. Character becomes destiny.

TOPIC OF MEETING	DAY / DATE

NOTES

ACTION ITEMS	DUE

Thoughts become words. Words become action. Actions become character. Character becomes destiny.

TOPIC OF MEETING	DAY / DATE

NOTES

ACTION ITEMS	DUE

Thoughts become words. Words become action. Actions become character. Character becomes destiny.

TOPIC OF MEETING	DAY / DATE

NOTES

ACTION ITEMS	DUE

Thoughts become words. Words become action. Actions become character. Character becomes destiny.

TOPIC OF MEETING	DAY / DATE

NOTES

ACTION ITEMS	DUE

Thoughts become words. Words become action. Actions become character. Character becomes destiny.

TOPIC OF MEETING	DAY / DATE

NOTES

ACTION ITEMS	DUE

Thoughts become words. Words become action. Actions become character. Character becomes destiny.

TOPIC OF MEETING	DAY / DATE

NOTES

ACTION ITEMS	DUE

Thoughts become words. Words become action. Actions become character. Character becomes destiny.

TOPIC OF MEETING	DAY / DATE

NOTES

ACTION ITEMS	DUE

Thoughts become words. Words become action. Actions become character. Character becomes destiny.

TOPIC OF MEETING	DAY / DATE

NOTES

ACTION ITEMS	DUE

TOPIC OF MEETING	DAY / DATE

NOTES

ACTION ITEMS	DUE

Thoughts become words. Words become action. Actions become character. Character becomes destiny.

TOPIC OF MEETING	DAY / DATE

NOTES

ACTION ITEMS	DUE

Thoughts become words. Words become action. Actions become character. Character becomes destiny.

TOPIC OF MEETING	DAY / DATE

NOTES

ACTION ITEMS	DUE

Thoughts become words. Words become action. Actions become character. Character becomes destiny.

TOPIC OF MEETING	DAY / DATE

NOTES

ACTION ITEMS	DUE

Thoughts become words. Words become action. Actions become character. Character becomes destiny.

TOPIC OF MEETING	DAY / DATE

NOTES

ACTION ITEMS	DUE

Thoughts become words. Words become action. Actions become character. Character becomes destiny.

TOPIC OF MEETING	DAY / DATE

NOTES

ACTION ITEMS	DUE

Thoughts become words. Words become action. Actions become character. Character becomes destiny.

TOPIC OF MEETING	DAY / DATE

NOTES

ACTION ITEMS	DUE

Thoughts become words. Words become action. Actions become character. Character becomes destiny.

TOPIC OF MEETING	DAY / DATE

NOTES

ACTION ITEMS	DUE

Thoughts become words. Words become action. Actions become character. Character becomes destiny.

TOPIC OF MEETING	DAY / DATE

NOTES

ACTION ITEMS	DUE

Thoughts become words. Words become action. Actions become character. Character becomes destiny.

TOPIC OF MEETING	DAY / DATE

NOTES

ACTION ITEMS	DUE

Thoughts become words. Words become action. Actions become character. Character becomes destiny.

TOPIC OF MEETING	DAY / DATE

NOTES

ACTION ITEMS	DUE

Thoughts become words. Words become action. Actions become character. Character becomes destiny.

TOPIC OF MEETING	DAY / DATE

NOTES

ACTION ITEMS	DUE

Thoughts become words. Words become action. Actions become character. Character becomes destiny.

TOPIC OF MEETING	DAY / DATE

NOTES

ACTION ITEMS	DUE

Thoughts become words. Words become action. Actions become character. Character becomes destiny.

TOPIC OF MEETING	DAY / DATE

NOTES

ACTION ITEMS	DUE

Thoughts become words. Words become action. Actions become character. Character becomes destiny.

TOPIC OF MEETING	DAY / DATE

NOTES

ACTION ITEMS	DUE

Thoughts become words. Words become action. Actions become character. Character becomes destiny.

TOPIC OF MEETING	DAY / DATE

NOTES

ACTION ITEMS	DUE

Thoughts become words. Words become action. Actions become character. Character becomes destiny.

TOPIC OF MEETING	DAY / DATE

NOTES

ACTION ITEMS	DUE

Thoughts become words. Words become action. Actions become character. Character becomes destiny.

TOPIC OF MEETING	DAY / DATE

NOTES

ACTION ITEMS	DUE

Thoughts become words. Words become action. Actions become character. Character becomes destiny.

TOPIC OF MEETING	DAY / DATE

NOTES

ACTION ITEMS	DUE

Thoughts become words. Words become action. Actions become character. Character becomes destiny.

TOPIC OF MEETING	DAY / DATE

NOTES

ACTION ITEMS	DUE

Thoughts become words. Words become action. Actions become character. Character becomes destiny.

TOPIC OF MEETING	DAY / DATE

NOTES

ACTION ITEMS	DUE

Thoughts become words. Words become action. Actions become character. Character becomes destiny.

TOPIC OF MEETING	DAY / DATE

NOTES

ACTION ITEMS	DUE

Thoughts become words. Words become action. Actions become character. Character becomes destiny.

TOPIC OF MEETING	DAY / DATE

NOTES

ACTION ITEMS	DUE

Thoughts become words. Words become action. Actions become character. Character becomes destiny.

TOPIC OF MEETING	DAY / DATE

NOTES

ACTION ITEMS	DUE

TOPIC OF MEETING	DAY / DATE

NOTES

ACTION ITEMS	DUE

Thoughts become words. Words become action. Actions become character. Character becomes destiny.

TOPIC OF MEETING	DAY / DATE

NOTES

ACTION ITEMS	DUE

Thoughts become words. Words become action. Actions become character. Character becomes destiny.

TOPIC OF MEETING	DAY / DATE

NOTES

ACTION ITEMS	DUE

Thoughts become words. Words become action. Actions become character. Character becomes destiny.

TOPIC OF MEETING	DAY / DATE

NOTES

ACTION ITEMS	DUE

Thoughts become words. Words become action. Actions become character. Character becomes destiny.

TOPIC OF MEETING	DAY / DATE

NOTES

ACTION ITEMS	DUE

Thoughts become words. Words become action. Actions become character. Character becomes destiny.

TOPIC OF MEETING	DAY / DATE

NOTES

ACTION ITEMS	DUE

Thoughts become words. Words become action. Actions become character. Character becomes destiny.

TOPIC OF MEETING	DAY / DATE

NOTES

ACTION ITEMS	DUE

Thoughts become words. Words become action. Actions become character. Character becomes destiny.

TOPIC OF MEETING	DAY / DATE

NOTES

ACTION ITEMS	DUE

Thoughts become words. Words become action. Actions become character. Character becomes destiny.

TOPIC OF MEETING	DAY / DATE

NOTES

ACTION ITEMS	DUE

Thoughts become words. Words become action. Actions become character. Character becomes destiny.

TOPIC OF MEETING	DAY / DATE

NOTES

ACTION ITEMS	DUE

Thoughts become words. Words become action. Actions become character. Character becomes destiny.

TOPIC OF MEETING	DAY / DATE

NOTES

ACTION ITEMS	DUE

Thoughts become words. Words become action. Actions become character. Character becomes destiny.

TOPIC OF MEETING	DAY / DATE

NOTES

ACTION ITEMS	DUE

Thoughts become words. Words become action. Actions become character. Character becomes destiny.

TOPIC OF MEETING	DAY / DATE

NOTES

ACTION ITEMS	DUE

Thoughts become words. Words become action. Actions become character. Character becomes destiny.

TOPIC OF MEETING	DAY / DATE

NOTES

ACTION ITEMS	DUE

Thoughts become words. Words become action. Actions become character. Character becomes destiny.

TOPIC OF MEETING	DAY / DATE

NOTES

ACTION ITEMS	DUE

Thoughts become words. Words become action. Actions become character. Character becomes destiny.

TOPIC OF MEETING	DAY / DATE

NOTES

ACTION ITEMS	DUE

Thoughts become words. Words become action. Actions become character. Character becomes destiny.

TOPIC OF MEETING	DAY / DATE

NOTES

ACTION ITEMS	DUE

Thoughts become words. Words become action. Actions become character. Character becomes destiny.

TOPIC OF MEETING	DAY / DATE

NOTES

ACTION ITEMS	DUE

Thoughts become words. Words become action. Actions become character. Character becomes destiny.

TOPIC OF MEETING	DAY / DATE

NOTES

ACTION ITEMS	DUE

Thoughts become words. Words become action. Actions become character. Character becomes destiny.

TOPIC OF MEETING	DAY / DATE

NOTES

ACTION ITEMS	DUE

Thoughts become words. Words become action. Actions become character. Character becomes destiny.

TOPIC OF MEETING	DAY / DATE

NOTES

ACTION ITEMS	DUE

Thoughts become words. Words become action. Actions become character. Character becomes destiny.

TOPIC OF MEETING	DAY / DATE

NOTES

ACTION ITEMS	DUE

Thoughts become words. Words become action. Actions become character. Character becomes destiny.

TOPIC OF MEETING	DAY / DATE

NOTES

ACTION ITEMS	DUE

Thoughts become words. Words become action. Actions become character. Character becomes destiny.

TOPIC OF MEETING	DAY / DATE

NOTES

ACTION ITEMS	DUE

Thoughts become words. Words become action. Actions become character. Character becomes destiny.

TOPIC OF MEETING	DAY / DATE

NOTES

ACTION ITEMS	DUE

Thoughts become words. Words become action. Actions become character. Character becomes destiny.

TOPIC OF MEETING	DAY / DATE

NOTES

ACTION ITEMS	DUE

Thoughts become words. Words become action. Actions become character. Character becomes destiny.

TOPIC OF MEETING	DAY / DATE

NOTES

ACTION ITEMS	DUE

Thoughts become words. Words become action. Actions become character. Character becomes destiny.

TOPIC OF MEETING	DAY / DATE

NOTES

ACTION ITEMS	DUE

Thoughts become words. Words become action. Actions become character. Character becomes destiny.

TOPIC OF MEETING	DAY / DATE

NOTES

ACTION ITEMS	DUE

Thoughts become words. Words become action. Actions become character. Character becomes destiny.

TOPIC OF MEETING	DAY / DATE

NOTES

ACTION ITEMS	DUE

Thoughts become words. Words become action. Actions become character. Character becomes destiny.

TOPIC OF MEETING	DAY / DATE

NOTES

ACTION ITEMS	DUE

Thoughts become words. Words become action. Actions become character. Character becomes destiny.

TOPIC OF MEETING	DAY / DATE

NOTES

ACTION ITEMS	DUE

Thoughts become words. Words become action. Actions become character. Character becomes destiny.

TOPIC OF MEETING	DAY / DATE

NOTES

ACTION ITEMS	DUE

Thoughts become words. Words become action. Actions become character. Character becomes destiny.

TOPIC OF MEETING	DAY / DATE

NOTES

ACTION ITEMS	DUE

TOPIC OF MEETING	DAY / DATE

NOTES

ACTION ITEMS	DUE

Thoughts become words. Words become action. Actions become character. Character becomes destiny.

TOPIC OF MEETING	DAY / DATE

NOTES

ACTION ITEMS	DUE

Thoughts become words. Words become action. Actions become character. Character becomes destiny.

TOPIC OF MEETING	DAY / DATE

NOTES

ACTION ITEMS	DUE

Thoughts become words. Words become action. Actions become character. Character becomes destiny.

TOPIC OF MEETING	DAY / DATE

NOTES

ACTION ITEMS	DUE

Thoughts become words. Words become action. Actions become character. Character becomes destiny.

TOPIC OF MEETING	DAY / DATE

NOTES

ACTION ITEMS	DUE

Thoughts become words. Words become action. Actions become character. Character becomes destiny.

TOPIC OF MEETING	DAY / DATE

NOTES

ACTION ITEMS	DUE

Thoughts become words. Words become action. Actions become character. Character becomes destiny.

TOPIC OF MEETING	DAY / DATE

NOTES

ACTION ITEMS	DUE

Thoughts become words. Words become action. Actions become character. Character becomes destiny.

TOPIC OF MEETING	DAY / DATE

NOTES

ACTION ITEMS	DUE

Thoughts become words. Words become action. Actions become character. Character becomes destiny.

TOPIC OF MEETING	DAY / DATE

NOTES

ACTION ITEMS	DUE

Thoughts become words. Words become action. Actions become character. Character becomes destiny.

TOPIC OF MEETING	DAY / DATE

NOTES

ACTION ITEMS	DUE

Thoughts become words. Words become action. Actions become character. Character becomes destiny.

TOPIC OF MEETING	DAY / DATE

NOTES

ACTION ITEMS	DUE

Thoughts become words. Words become action. Actions become character. Character becomes destiny.

TOPIC OF MEETING	DAY / DATE

NOTES

ACTION ITEMS	DUE

Thoughts become words. Words become action. Actions become character. Character becomes destiny.

TOPIC OF MEETING	DAY / DATE

NOTES

ACTION ITEMS	DUE

Thoughts become words. Words become action. Actions become character. Character becomes destiny.

TOPIC OF MEETING	DAY / DATE

NOTES

ACTION ITEMS	DUE

Thoughts become words. Words become action. Actions become character. Character becomes destiny.

TOPIC OF MEETING	DAY / DATE

NOTES

ACTION ITEMS	DUE

Thoughts become words. Words become action. Actions become character. Character becomes destiny.

TOPIC OF MEETING	DAY / DATE

NOTES

ACTION ITEMS	DUE

Thoughts become words. Words become action. Actions become character. Character becomes destiny.

TOPIC OF MEETING	DAY / DATE

NOTES

ACTION ITEMS	DUE

Thoughts become words. Words become action. Actions become character. Character becomes destiny.

TOPIC OF MEETING	DAY / DATE

NOTES

ACTION ITEMS	DUE

Thoughts become words. Words become action. Actions become character. Character becomes destiny.

TOPIC OF MEETING	DAY / DATE

NOTES

ACTION ITEMS	DUE

Thoughts become words. Words become action. Actions become character. Character becomes destiny.

TOPIC OF MEETING	DAY / DATE

NOTES

ACTION ITEMS	DUE

Thoughts become words. Words become action. Actions become character. Character becomes destiny.

TOPIC OF MEETING	DAY / DATE

NOTES

ACTION ITEMS	DUE

Thoughts become words. Words become action. Actions become character. Character becomes destiny.

TOPIC OF MEETING	DAY / DATE

NOTES

ACTION ITEMS	DUE

Thoughts become words. Words become action. Actions become character. Character becomes destiny.

TOPIC OF MEETING	DAY / DATE

NOTES

ACTION ITEMS	DUE

Thoughts become words. Words become action. Actions become character. Character becomes destiny.

TOPIC OF MEETING	DAY / DATE

NOTES

ACTION ITEMS	DUE

Thoughts become words. Words become action. Actions become character. Character becomes destiny.

TOPIC OF MEETING	DAY / DATE

NOTES

ACTION ITEMS	DUE

Thoughts become words. Words become action. Actions become character. Character becomes destiny.

TOPIC OF MEETING	DAY / DATE

NOTES

ACTION ITEMS	DUE

Thoughts become words. Words become action. Actions become character. Character becomes destiny.

TOPIC OF MEETING	DAY / DATE

NOTES

ACTION ITEMS	DUE

Thoughts become words. Words become action. Actions become character. Character becomes destiny.

TOPIC OF MEETING	DAY / DATE

NOTES

ACTION ITEMS	DUE

Thoughts become words. Words become action. Actions become character. Character becomes destiny.

TOPIC OF MEETING	DAY / DATE

NOTES

ACTION ITEMS	DUE

Thoughts become words. Words become action. Actions become character. Character becomes destiny.

TOPIC OF MEETING	DAY / DATE

NOTES

ACTION ITEMS	DUE

Thoughts become words. Words become action. Actions become character. Character becomes destiny.

TOPIC OF MEETING	DAY / DATE

NOTES

ACTION ITEMS	DUE

Thoughts become words. Words become action. Actions become character. Character becomes destiny.

TOPIC OF MEETING	DAY / DATE

NOTES

ACTION ITEMS	DUE

Thoughts become words. Words become action. Actions become character. Character becomes destiny.

TOPIC OF MEETING	DAY / DATE

NOTES

ACTION ITEMS	DUE

Thoughts become words. Words become action. Actions become character. Character becomes destiny.

TOPIC OF MEETING	DAY / DATE

NOTES

ACTION ITEMS	DUE

Thoughts become words. Words become action. Actions become character. Character becomes destiny.

TOPIC OF MEETING	DAY / DATE

NOTES

ACTION ITEMS	DUE

TOPIC OF MEETING	DAY / DATE

NOTES

ACTION ITEMS	DUE

Thoughts become words. Words become action. Actions become character. Character becomes destiny.

TOPIC OF MEETING	DAY / DATE

NOTES

ACTION ITEMS	DUE

Thoughts become words. Words become action. Actions become character. Character becomes destiny.

TOPIC OF MEETING	DAY / DATE

NOTES

ACTION ITEMS	DUE

Thoughts become words. Words become action. Actions become character. Character becomes destiny.

TOPIC OF MEETING	DAY / DATE

NOTES

ACTION ITEMS	DUE

Thoughts become words. Words become action. Actions become character. Character becomes destiny.

TOPIC OF MEETING	DAY / DATE

NOTES

ACTION ITEMS	DUE

Thoughts become words. Words become action. Actions become character. Character becomes destiny.

TOPIC OF MEETING	DAY / DATE

NOTES

ACTION ITEMS	DUE

Thoughts become words. Words become action. Actions become character. Character becomes destiny.

TOPIC OF MEETING	DAY / DATE

NOTES

ACTION ITEMS	DUE

Thoughts become words. Words become action. Actions become character. Character becomes destiny.

TOPIC OF MEETING	DAY / DATE

NOTES

ACTION ITEMS	DUE

Thoughts become words. Words become action. Actions become character. Character becomes destiny.

TOPIC OF MEETING	DAY / DATE

NOTES

ACTION ITEMS	DUE

TOPIC OF MEETING	DAY / DATE

NOTES

ACTION ITEMS	DUE

Thoughts become words. Words become action. Actions become character. Character becomes destiny.

TOPIC OF MEETING	DAY / DATE

NOTES

ACTION ITEMS	DUE

Thoughts become words. Words become action. Actions become character. Character becomes destiny.

TOPIC OF MEETING	DAY / DATE

NOTES

ACTION ITEMS	DUE

Thoughts become words. Words become action. Actions become character. Character becomes destiny.

TOPIC OF MEETING	DAY / DATE

NOTES

ACTION ITEMS	DUE

Thoughts become words. Words become action. Actions become character. Character becomes destiny.

TOPIC OF MEETING	DAY / DATE

NOTES

ACTION ITEMS	DUE

Thoughts become words. Words become action. Actions become character. Character becomes destiny.

TOPIC OF MEETING	DAY / DATE

NOTES

ACTION ITEMS	DUE

Thoughts become words. Words become action. Actions become character. Character becomes destiny.

TOPIC OF MEETING	DAY / DATE

NOTES

ACTION ITEMS	DUE

Thoughts become words. Words become action. Actions become character. Character becomes destiny.

TOPIC OF MEETING	DAY / DATE

NOTES

ACTION ITEMS	DUE

Thoughts become words. Words become action. Actions become character. Character becomes destiny.

TOPIC OF MEETING	DAY / DATE

NOTES

ACTION ITEMS	DUE

Thoughts become words. Words become action. Actions become character. Character becomes destiny.

TOPIC OF MEETING	DAY / DATE

NOTES

ACTION ITEMS	DUE

Thoughts become words. Words become action. Actions become character. Character becomes destiny.

TOPIC OF MEETING	DAY / DATE

NOTES

ACTION ITEMS	DUE

Thoughts become words. Words become action. Actions become character. Character becomes destiny.

TOPIC OF MEETING	DAY / DATE

NOTES

ACTION ITEMS	DUE

Thoughts become words. Words become action. Actions become character. Character becomes destiny.

TOPIC OF MEETING	DAY / DATE

NOTES

ACTION ITEMS	DUE

Thoughts become words. Words become action. Actions become character. Character becomes destiny.

TOPIC OF MEETING	DAY / DATE

NOTES

ACTION ITEMS	DUE

TOPIC OF MEETING	DAY / DATE

NOTES

ACTION ITEMS	DUE

Thoughts become words. Words become action. Actions become character. Character becomes destiny.

TOPIC OF MEETING	DAY / DATE

NOTES

ACTION ITEMS	DUE

Thoughts become words. Words become action. Actions become character. Character becomes destiny.

TOPIC OF MEETING	DAY / DATE

NOTES

ACTION ITEMS	DUE

Thoughts become words. Words become action. Actions become character. Character becomes destiny.

TOPIC OF MEETING	DAY / DATE

NOTES

ACTION ITEMS	DUE

Thoughts become words. Words become action. Actions become character. Character becomes destiny.

TOPIC OF MEETING	DAY / DATE

NOTES

ACTION ITEMS	DUE

Thoughts become words. Words become action. Actions become character. Character becomes destiny.

TOPIC OF MEETING	DAY / DATE

NOTES

ACTION ITEMS	DUE

Thoughts become words. Words become action. Actions become character. Character becomes destiny.

TOPIC OF MEETING	DAY / DATE

NOTES

ACTION ITEMS	DUE

Thoughts become words. Words become action. Actions become character. Character becomes destiny.

TOPIC OF MEETING	DAY / DATE

NOTES

ACTION ITEMS	DUE

Thoughts become words. Words become action. Actions become character. Character becomes destiny.

TOPIC OF MEETING	DAY / DATE

NOTES

ACTION ITEMS	DUE

Thoughts become words. Words become action. Actions become character. Character becomes destiny.

TOPIC OF MEETING	DAY / DATE

NOTES

ACTION ITEMS	DUE

Thoughts become words. Words become action. Actions become character. Character becomes destiny.

TOPIC OF MEETING	DAY / DATE

NOTES

ACTION ITEMS	DUE

Thoughts become words. Words become action. Actions become character. Character becomes destiny.

TOPIC OF MEETING	DAY / DATE

NOTES

ACTION ITEMS	DUE

Thoughts become words. Words become action. Actions become character. Character becomes destiny.

TOPIC OF MEETING	DAY / DATE

NOTES

ACTION ITEMS	DUE

Thoughts become words. Words become action. Actions become character. Character becomes destiny.

TOPIC OF MEETING	DAY / DATE

NOTES

ACTION ITEMS	DUE

Thoughts become words. Words become action. Actions become character. Character becomes destiny.

TOPIC OF MEETING	DAY / DATE

NOTES

ACTION ITEMS	DUE

Thoughts become words. Words become action. Actions become character. Character becomes destiny.

TOPIC OF MEETING	DAY / DATE

NOTES

ACTION ITEMS	DUE

Thoughts become words. Words become action. Actions become character. Character becomes destiny.

TOPIC OF MEETING	DAY / DATE

NOTES

ACTION ITEMS	DUE

Thoughts become words. Words become action. Actions become character. Character becomes destiny.

TOPIC OF MEETING	DAY / DATE

NOTES

ACTION ITEMS	DUE

Thoughts become words. Words become action. Actions become character. Character becomes destiny.

TOPIC OF MEETING	DAY / DATE

NOTES

ACTION ITEMS	DUE

Thoughts become words. Words become action. Actions become character. Character becomes destiny.

TOPIC OF MEETING	DAY / DATE

NOTES

ACTION ITEMS	DUE

Thoughts become words. Words become action. Actions become character. Character becomes destiny.

TOPIC OF MEETING	DAY / DATE

NOTES

ACTION ITEMS	DUE

Thoughts become words. Words become action. Actions become character. Character becomes destiny.

TOPIC OF MEETING	DAY / DATE

NOTES

ACTION ITEMS	DUE

Thoughts become words. Words become action. Actions become character. Character becomes destiny.

TOPIC OF MEETING	DAY / DATE

NOTES

ACTION ITEMS	DUE

Thoughts become words. Words become action. Actions become character. Character becomes destiny.

TOPIC OF MEETING	DAY / DATE

NOTES

ACTION ITEMS	DUE

Thoughts become words. Words become action. Actions become character. Character becomes destiny.

TOPIC OF MEETING	DAY / DATE

NOTES

ACTION ITEMS	DUE

Thoughts become words. Words become action. Actions become character. Character becomes destiny.

TOPIC OF MEETING	DAY / DATE

NOTES

ACTION ITEMS	DUE

Thoughts become words. Words become action. Actions become character. Character becomes destiny.

TOPIC OF MEETING	DAY / DATE

NOTES

ACTION ITEMS	DUE

Thoughts become words. Words become action. Actions become character. Character becomes destiny.

TOPIC OF MEETING	DAY / DATE

NOTES

ACTION ITEMS	DUE

Thoughts become words. Words become action. Actions become character. Character becomes destiny.

TOPIC OF MEETING	DAY / DATE

NOTES

ACTION ITEMS	DUE

Thoughts become words. Words become action. Actions become character. Character becomes destiny.

TOPIC OF MEETING	DAY / DATE

NOTES

ACTION ITEMS	DUE

Thoughts become words. Words become action. Actions become character. Character becomes destiny.

TOPIC OF MEETING	DAY / DATE

NOTES

ACTION ITEMS	DUE

Thoughts become words. Words become action. Actions become character. Character becomes destiny.

TOPIC OF MEETING	DAY / DATE

NOTES

ACTION ITEMS	DUE

Thoughts become words. Words become action. Actions become character. Character becomes destiny.

TOPIC OF MEETING	DAY / DATE

NOTES

ACTION ITEMS	DUE

Thoughts become words. Words become action. Actions become character. Character becomes destiny.

TOPIC OF MEETING	DAY / DATE

NOTES

ACTION ITEMS	DUE

Thoughts become words. Words become action. Actions become character. Character becomes destiny.

TOPIC OF MEETING	DAY / DATE

NOTES

ACTION ITEMS	DUE

Thoughts become words. Words become action. Actions become character. Character becomes destiny.

TOPIC OF MEETING	DAY / DATE

NOTES

ACTION ITEMS	DUE

Thoughts become words. Words become action. Actions become character. Character becomes destiny.

TOPIC OF MEETING	DAY / DATE

NOTES

ACTION ITEMS	DUE

Thoughts become words. Words become action. Actions become character. Character becomes destiny.

TOPIC OF MEETING	DAY / DATE

NOTES

ACTION ITEMS	DUE

Thoughts become words. Words become action. Actions become character. Character becomes destiny.

TOPIC OF MEETING	DAY / DATE

NOTES

ACTION ITEMS	DUE

Thoughts become words. Words become action. Actions become character. Character becomes destiny.

TOPIC OF MEETING	DAY / DATE

NOTES

ACTION ITEMS	DUE

Thoughts become words. Words become action. Actions become character. Character becomes destiny.

TOPIC OF MEETING	DAY / DATE

NOTES

ACTION ITEMS	DUE

Thoughts become words. Words become action. Actions become character. Character becomes destiny.

TOPIC OF MEETING	DAY / DATE

NOTES

ACTION ITEMS	DUE

Thoughts become words. Words become action. Actions become character. Character becomes destiny.

TOPIC OF MEETING	DAY / DATE

NOTES

ACTION ITEMS	DUE

Thoughts become words. Words become action. Actions become character. Character becomes destiny.

TOPIC OF MEETING	DAY / DATE

NOTES

ACTION ITEMS	DUE

Thoughts become words. Words become action. Actions become character. Character becomes destiny.

TOPIC OF MEETING	DAY / DATE

NOTES

ACTION ITEMS	DUE

Thoughts become words. Words become action. Actions become character. Character becomes destiny.

TOPIC OF MEETING	DAY / DATE

NOTES

ACTION ITEMS	DUE

Thoughts become words. Words become action. Actions become character. Character becomes destiny.

TOPIC OF MEETING	DAY / DATE

NOTES

ACTION ITEMS	DUE

Thoughts become words. Words become action. Actions become character. Character becomes destiny.

TOPIC OF MEETING	DAY / DATE

NOTES

ACTION ITEMS	DUE

Thoughts become words. Words become action. Actions become character. Character becomes destiny.

TOPIC OF MEETING	DAY / DATE

NOTES

ACTION ITEMS	DUE

Thoughts become words. Words become action. Actions become character. Character becomes destiny.

TOPIC OF MEETING	DAY / DATE

NOTES

ACTION ITEMS	DUE

Thoughts become words. Words become action. Actions become character. Character becomes destiny.

TOPIC OF MEETING	DAY / DATE

NOTES

ACTION ITEMS	DUE

Thoughts become words. Words become action. Actions become character. Character becomes destiny.

TOPIC OF MEETING	DAY / DATE

NOTES

ACTION ITEMS	DUE

Thoughts become words. Words become action. Actions become character. Character becomes destiny.

TOPIC OF MEETING	DAY / DATE

NOTES

ACTION ITEMS	DUE

Thoughts become words. Words become action. Actions become character. Character becomes destiny.

TOPIC OF MEETING	DAY / DATE

NOTES

ACTION ITEMS	DUE

Thoughts become words. Words become action. Actions become character. Character becomes destiny.

TOPIC OF MEETING	DAY / DATE

NOTES

ACTION ITEMS	DUE

Thoughts become words. Words become action. Actions become character. Character becomes destiny.

TOPIC OF MEETING	DAY / DATE

NOTES

ACTION ITEMS	DUE

TOPIC OF MEETING	DAY / DATE

NOTES

ACTION ITEMS	DUE

Thoughts become words. Words become action. Actions become character. Character becomes destiny.

TOPIC OF MEETING	DAY / DATE

NOTES

ACTION ITEMS	DUE

Thoughts become words. Words become action. Actions become character. Character becomes destiny.

TOPIC OF MEETING	DAY / DATE

NOTES

ACTION ITEMS	DUE

Thoughts become words. Words become action. Actions become character. Character becomes destiny.

TOPIC OF MEETING	DAY / DATE

NOTES

ACTION ITEMS	DUE

Thoughts become words. Words become action. Actions become character. Character becomes destiny.

TOPIC OF MEETING	DAY / DATE

NOTES

ACTION ITEMS	DUE

Thoughts become words. Words become action. Actions become character. Character becomes destiny.

TOPIC OF MEETING	DAY / DATE

NOTES

ACTION ITEMS	DUE

Thoughts become words. Words become action. Actions become character. Character becomes destiny.

TOPIC OF MEETING	DAY / DATE

NOTES

ACTION ITEMS	DUE

Thoughts become words. Words become action. Actions become character. Character becomes destiny.

TOPIC OF MEETING	DAY / DATE

NOTES

ACTION ITEMS	DUE

Thoughts become words. Words become action. Actions become character. Character becomes destiny.

TOPIC OF MEETING	DAY / DATE

NOTES

ACTION ITEMS	DUE

Thoughts become words. Words become action. Actions become character. Character becomes destiny.

TOPIC OF MEETING	DAY / DATE

NOTES

ACTION ITEMS	DUE

Thoughts become words. Words become action. Actions become character. Character becomes destiny.

TOPIC OF MEETING	DAY / DATE

NOTES

ACTION ITEMS	DUE

Thoughts become words. Words become action. Actions become character. Character becomes destiny.

TOPIC OF MEETING	DAY / DATE

NOTES

ACTION ITEMS	DUE

Thoughts become words. Words become action. Actions become character. Character becomes destiny.

TOPIC OF MEETING	DAY / DATE

NOTES

ACTION ITEMS	DUE

Thoughts become words. Words become action. Actions become character. Character becomes destiny.

TOPIC OF MEETING	DAY / DATE

NOTES

ACTION ITEMS	DUE

Thoughts become words. Words become action. Actions become character. Character becomes destiny.

TOPIC OF MEETING	DAY / DATE

NOTES

ACTION ITEMS	DUE

TOPIC OF MEETING	DAY / DATE

NOTES

ACTION ITEMS	DUE

Thoughts become words. Words become action. Actions become character. Character becomes destiny.

TOPIC OF MEETING	DAY / DATE

NOTES

ACTION ITEMS	DUE

Thoughts become words. Words become action. Actions become character. Character becomes destiny.

TOPIC OF MEETING	DAY / DATE

NOTES

ACTION ITEMS	DUE

Thoughts become words. Words become action. Actions become character. Character becomes destiny.

TOPIC OF MEETING	DAY / DATE

NOTES

ACTION ITEMS	DUE

Thoughts become words. Words become action. Actions become character. Character becomes destiny.

TOPIC OF MEETING	DAY / DATE

NOTES

ACTION ITEMS	DUE

Thoughts become words. Words become action. Actions become character. Character becomes destiny.

TOPIC OF MEETING	DAY / DATE

NOTES

ACTION ITEMS	DUE

Thoughts become words. Words become action. Actions become character. Character becomes destiny.

TOPIC OF MEETING	DAY / DATE

NOTES

ACTION ITEMS	DUE

Thoughts become words. Words become action. Actions become character. Character becomes destiny.

TOPIC OF MEETING	DAY / DATE

NOTES

ACTION ITEMS	DUE

Thoughts become words. Words become action. Actions become character. Character becomes destiny.

TOPIC OF MEETING	DAY / DATE

NOTES

ACTION ITEMS	DUE

Thoughts become words. Words become action. Actions become character. Character becomes destiny.

TOPIC OF MEETING	DAY / DATE

NOTES

ACTION ITEMS	DUE

Thoughts become words. Words become action. Actions become character. Character becomes destiny.

TOPIC OF MEETING	DAY / DATE

NOTES

ACTION ITEMS	DUE

TOPIC OF MEETING	DAY / DATE

NOTES

ACTION ITEMS	DUE

TOPIC OF MEETING	DAY / DATE

NOTES

ACTION ITEMS	DUE

Thoughts become words. Words become action. Actions become character. Character becomes destiny.

TOPIC OF MEETING	DAY / DATE

NOTES

ACTION ITEMS	DUE

Thoughts become words. Words become action. Actions become character. Character becomes destiny.

TOPIC OF MEETING	DAY / DATE

NOTES

ACTION ITEMS	DUE

Thoughts become words. Words become action. Actions become character. Character becomes destiny.

TOPIC OF MEETING	DAY / DATE

NOTES

ACTION ITEMS	DUE

Thoughts become words. Words become action. Actions become character. Character becomes destiny.

TOPIC OF MEETING	DAY / DATE

NOTES

ACTION ITEMS	DUE

Thoughts become words. Words become action. Actions become character. Character becomes destiny.

TOPIC OF MEETING	DAY / DATE

NOTES

ACTION ITEMS	DUE

Thoughts become words. Words become action. Actions become character. Character becomes destiny.

TOPIC OF MEETING	DAY / DATE

NOTES

ACTION ITEMS	DUE

TOPIC OF MEETING	DAY / DATE

NOTES

ACTION ITEMS	DUE

Thoughts become words. Words become action. Actions become character. Character becomes destiny.

TOPIC OF MEETING	DAY / DATE

NOTES

ACTION ITEMS	DUE

Thoughts become words. Words become action. Actions become character. Character becomes destiny.

TOPIC OF MEETING	DAY / DATE

NOTES

ACTION ITEMS	DUE

Thoughts become words. Words become action. Actions become character. Character becomes destiny.

TOPIC OF MEETING	DAY / DATE

NOTES

ACTION ITEMS	DUE

Thoughts become words. Words become action. Actions become character. Character becomes destiny.

TOPIC OF MEETING	DAY / DATE

NOTES

ACTION ITEMS	DUE

Thoughts become words. Words become action. Actions become character. Character becomes destiny.

TOPIC OF MEETING	DAY / DATE

NOTES

ACTION ITEMS	DUE

Thoughts become words. Words become action. Actions become character. Character becomes destiny.

TOPIC OF MEETING	DAY / DATE

NOTES

ACTION ITEMS	DUE

Thoughts become words. Words become action. Actions become character. Character becomes destiny.

TOPIC OF MEETING	DAY / DATE

NOTES

ACTION ITEMS	DUE

TOPIC OF MEETING	DAY / DATE

NOTES

ACTION ITEMS	DUE

Thoughts become words. Words become action. Actions become character. Character becomes destiny.

TOPIC OF MEETING	DAY / DATE

NOTES

ACTION ITEMS	DUE

TOPIC OF MEETING	DAY / DATE

NOTES

ACTION ITEMS	DUE

Thoughts become words. Words become action. Actions become character. Character becomes destiny.

TOPIC OF MEETING	DAY / DATE

NOTES

ACTION ITEMS	DUE

TOPIC OF MEETING	DAY / DATE

NOTES

ACTION ITEMS	DUE

Thoughts become words. Words become action. Actions become character. Character becomes destiny.

TOPIC OF MEETING	DAY / DATE

NOTES

ACTION ITEMS	DUE

Thoughts become words. Words become action. Actions become character. Character becomes destiny.

TOPIC OF MEETING	DAY / DATE

NOTES

ACTION ITEMS	DUE

Thoughts become words. Words become action. Actions become character. Character becomes destiny.

TOPIC OF MEETING	DAY / DATE

NOTES

ACTION ITEMS	DUE

Thoughts become words. Words become action. Actions become character. Character becomes destiny.

TOPIC OF MEETING	DAY / DATE

NOTES

ACTION ITEMS	DUE

Thoughts become words. Words become action. Actions become character. Character becomes destiny.

TOPIC OF MEETING	DAY / DATE

NOTES

ACTION ITEMS	DUE

Thoughts become words. Words become action. Actions become character. Character becomes destiny.

TOPIC OF MEETING	DAY / DATE

NOTES

ACTION ITEMS	DUE

Thoughts become words. Words become action. Actions become character. Character becomes destiny.

TOPIC OF MEETING	DAY / DATE

NOTES

ACTION ITEMS	DUE

TOPIC OF MEETING	DAY / DATE

NOTES

ACTION ITEMS	DUE

Thoughts become words. Words become action. Actions become character. Character becomes destiny.

TOPIC OF MEETING	DAY / DATE

NOTES

ACTION ITEMS	DUE

Thoughts become words. Words become action. Actions become character. Character becomes destiny.

TOPIC OF MEETING	DAY / DATE

NOTES

ACTION ITEMS	DUE

Thoughts become words. Words become action. Actions become character. Character becomes destiny.

TOPIC OF MEETING	DAY / DATE

NOTES

ACTION ITEMS	DUE

Thoughts become words. Words become action. Actions become character. Character becomes destiny.

TOPIC OF MEETING	DAY / DATE

NOTES

ACTION ITEMS	DUE

Thoughts become words. Words become action. Actions become character. Character becomes destiny.

TOPIC OF MEETING	DAY / DATE

NOTES

ACTION ITEMS	DUE

Thoughts become words. Words become action. Actions become character. Character becomes destiny.

TOPIC OF MEETING	DAY / DATE

NOTES

ACTION ITEMS	DUE

Thoughts become words. Words become action. Actions become character. Character becomes destiny.

TOPIC OF MEETING	DAY / DATE

NOTES

ACTION ITEMS	DUE

Thoughts become words. Words become action. Actions become character. Character becomes destiny.

TOPIC OF MEETING	DAY / DATE

NOTES

ACTION ITEMS	DUE

Thoughts become words. Words become action. Actions become character. Character becomes destiny.

TOPIC OF MEETING	DAY / DATE

NOTES

ACTION ITEMS	DUE

Thoughts become words. Words become action. Actions become character. Character becomes destiny.

TOPIC OF MEETING	DAY / DATE

NOTES

ACTION ITEMS	DUE

Thoughts become words. Words become action. Actions become character. Character becomes destiny.

TOPIC OF MEETING	DAY / DATE

NOTES

ACTION ITEMS	DUE

Thoughts become words. Words become action. Actions become character. Character becomes destiny.

TOPIC OF MEETING	DAY / DATE

NOTES

ACTION ITEMS	DUE

Thoughts become words. Words become action. Actions become character. Character becomes destiny.

TOPIC OF MEETING	DAY / DATE

NOTES

ACTION ITEMS	DUE

TOPIC OF MEETING	DAY / DATE

NOTES

ACTION ITEMS	DUE

Thoughts become words. Words become action. Actions become character. Character becomes destiny.

TOPIC OF MEETING	DAY / DATE

NOTES

ACTION ITEMS	DUE

Thoughts become words. Words become action. Actions become character. Character becomes destiny.

TOPIC OF MEETING	DAY / DATE

NOTES

ACTION ITEMS	DUE

Thoughts become words. Words become action. Actions become character. Character becomes destiny.

TOPIC OF MEETING	DAY / DATE

NOTES

ACTION ITEMS	DUE

Thoughts become words. Words become action. Actions become character. Character becomes destiny.

TOPIC OF MEETING	DAY / DATE

NOTES

ACTION ITEMS	DUE

Thoughts become words. Words become action. Actions become character. Character becomes destiny.

TOPIC OF MEETING	DAY / DATE

NOTES

ACTION ITEMS	DUE

Thoughts become words. Words become action. Actions become character. Character becomes destiny.

TOPIC OF MEETING	DAY / DATE

NOTES

ACTION ITEMS	DUE

Thoughts become words. Words become action. Actions become character. Character becomes destiny.

TOPIC OF MEETING	DAY / DATE

NOTES

ACTION ITEMS	DUE

Thoughts become words. Words become action. Actions become character. Character becomes destiny.

TOPIC OF MEETING	DAY / DATE

NOTES

ACTION ITEMS	DUE

Thoughts become words. Words become action. Actions become character. Character becomes destiny.

TOPIC OF MEETING	DAY / DATE

NOTES

ACTION ITEMS	DUE

Thoughts become words. Words become action. Actions become character. Character becomes destiny.

TOPIC OF MEETING	DAY / DATE

NOTES

ACTION ITEMS	DUE

Thoughts become words. Words become action. Actions become character. Character becomes destiny.

TOPIC OF MEETING	DAY / DATE

NOTES

ACTION ITEMS	DUE

Thoughts become words. Words become action. Actions become character. Character becomes destiny.

TOPIC OF MEETING	DAY / DATE

NOTES

ACTION ITEMS	DUE

Thoughts become words. Words become action. Actions become character. Character becomes destiny.

TOPIC OF MEETING	DAY / DATE

NOTES

ACTION ITEMS	DUE

Thoughts become words. Words become action. Actions become character. Character becomes destiny.

TOPIC OF MEETING	DAY / DATE

NOTES

ACTION ITEMS	DUE

Thoughts become words. Words become action. Actions become character. Character becomes destiny.

TOPIC OF MEETING	DAY / DATE

NOTES

ACTION ITEMS	DUE

Thoughts become words. Words become action. Actions become character. Character becomes destiny.

TOPIC OF MEETING	DAY / DATE

NOTES

ACTION ITEMS	DUE

Thoughts become words. Words become action. Actions become character. Character becomes destiny.

TOPIC OF MEETING	DAY / DATE

NOTES

ACTION ITEMS	DUE

Thoughts become words. Words become action. Actions become character. Character becomes destiny.

TOPIC OF MEETING	DAY / DATE

NOTES

ACTION ITEMS	DUE

Thoughts become words. Words become action. Actions become character. Character becomes destiny.

TOPIC OF MEETING	DAY / DATE

NOTES

ACTION ITEMS	DUE

Thoughts become words. Words become action. Actions become character. Character becomes destiny.

TOPIC OF MEETING	DAY / DATE

NOTES

ACTION ITEMS	DUE

TOPIC OF MEETING	DAY / DATE

NOTES

ACTION ITEMS	DUE

Thoughts become words. Words become action. Actions become character. Character becomes destiny.

TOPIC OF MEETING	DAY / DATE

NOTES

ACTION ITEMS	DUE

Thoughts become words. Words become action. Actions become character. Character becomes destiny.

TOPIC OF MEETING	DAY / DATE

NOTES

ACTION ITEMS	DUE

Thoughts become words. Words become action. Actions become character. Character becomes destiny.

TOPIC OF MEETING	DAY / DATE

NOTES

ACTION ITEMS	DUE

Thoughts become words. Words become action. Actions become character. Character becomes destiny.

TOPIC OF MEETING	DAY / DATE

NOTES

ACTION ITEMS	DUE

Thoughts become words. Words become action. Actions become character. Character becomes destiny.

TOPIC OF MEETING	DAY / DATE

NOTES

ACTION ITEMS	DUE

Thoughts become words. Words become action. Actions become character. Character becomes destiny.

TOPIC OF MEETING	DAY / DATE

NOTES

ACTION ITEMS	DUE

Thoughts become words. Words become action. Actions become character. Character becomes destiny.

TOPIC OF MEETING	DAY / DATE

NOTES

ACTION ITEMS	DUE

Thoughts become words. Words become action. Actions become character. Character becomes destiny.

TOPIC OF MEETING	DAY / DATE

NOTES

ACTION ITEMS	DUE

Thoughts become words. Words become action. Actions become character. Character becomes destiny.

TOPIC OF MEETING	DAY / DATE

NOTES

ACTION ITEMS	DUE

Thoughts become words. Words become action. Actions become character. Character becomes destiny.

TOPIC OF MEETING	DAY / DATE

NOTES

ACTION ITEMS	DUE

Thoughts become words. Words become action. Actions become character. Character becomes destiny.

TOPIC OF MEETING	DAY / DATE

NOTES

ACTION ITEMS	DUE

Thoughts become words. Words become action. Actions become character. Character becomes destiny.

TOPIC OF MEETING	DAY / DATE

NOTES

ACTION ITEMS	DUE

Thoughts become words. Words become action. Actions become character. Character becomes destiny.

TOPIC OF MEETING	DAY / DATE

NOTES

ACTION ITEMS	DUE

Thoughts become words. Words become action. Actions become character. Character becomes destiny.

TOPIC OF MEETING	DAY / DATE

NOTES

ACTION ITEMS	DUE

Thoughts become words. Words become action. Actions become character. Character becomes destiny.

TOPIC OF MEETING	DAY / DATE

NOTES

ACTION ITEMS	DUE

Thoughts become words. Words become action. Actions become character. Character becomes destiny.

TOPIC OF MEETING	DAY / DATE

NOTES

ACTION ITEMS	DUE

Thoughts become words. Words become action. Actions become character. Character becomes destiny.

TOPIC OF MEETING	DAY / DATE

NOTES

ACTION ITEMS	DUE

Thoughts become words. Words become action. Actions become character. Character becomes destiny.

TOPIC OF MEETING	DAY / DATE

NOTES

ACTION ITEMS	DUE

Thoughts become words. Words become action. Actions become character. Character becomes destiny.

TOPIC OF MEETING	DAY / DATE

NOTES

ACTION ITEMS	DUE

Thoughts become words. Words become action. Actions become character. Character becomes destiny.

TOPIC OF MEETING	DAY / DATE

NOTES

ACTION ITEMS	DUE

Thoughts become words. Words become action. Actions become character. Character becomes destiny.

TOPIC OF MEETING	DAY / DATE

NOTES

ACTION ITEMS	DUE

Thoughts become words. Words become action. Actions become character. Character becomes destiny.

TOPIC OF MEETING	DAY / DATE

NOTES

ACTION ITEMS	DUE

Thoughts become words. Words become action. Actions become character. Character becomes destiny.

TOPIC OF MEETING	DAY / DATE

NOTES

ACTION ITEMS	DUE

Thoughts become words. Words become action. Actions become character. Character becomes destiny.

TOPIC OF MEETING	DAY / DATE

NOTES

ACTION ITEMS	DUE

Thoughts become words. Words become action. Actions become character. Character becomes destiny.

TOPIC OF MEETING	DAY / DATE

NOTES

ACTION ITEMS	DUE

Thoughts become words. Words become action. Actions become character. Character becomes destiny.

TOPIC OF MEETING	DAY / DATE

NOTES

ACTION ITEMS	DUE

Thoughts become words. Words become action. Actions become character. Character becomes destiny.

TOPIC OF MEETING	DAY / DATE

NOTES

ACTION ITEMS	DUE

Thoughts become words. Words become action. Actions become character. Character becomes destiny.

TOPIC OF MEETING	DAY / DATE

NOTES

ACTION ITEMS	DUE

Thoughts become words. Words become action. Actions become character. Character becomes destiny.

TOPIC OF MEETING	DAY / DATE

NOTES

ACTION ITEMS	DUE

Thoughts become words. Words become action. Actions become character. Character becomes destiny.

TOPIC OF MEETING	DAY / DATE

NOTES

ACTION ITEMS	DUE

Thoughts become words. Words become action. Actions become character. Character becomes destiny.

TOPIC OF MEETING	DAY / DATE

NOTES

ACTION ITEMS	DUE

Thoughts become words. Words become action. Actions become character. Character becomes destiny.

TOPIC OF MEETING	DAY / DATE

NOTES

ACTION ITEMS	DUE

Thoughts become words. Words become action. Actions become character. Character becomes destiny.

TOPIC OF MEETING	DAY / DATE

NOTES

ACTION ITEMS	DUE

Thoughts become words. Words become action. Actions become character. Character becomes destiny.

TOPIC OF MEETING	DAY / DATE

NOTES

ACTION ITEMS	DUE

Thoughts become words. Words become action. Actions become character. Character becomes destiny.

TOPIC OF MEETING	DAY / DATE

NOTES

ACTION ITEMS	DUE

Thoughts become words. Words become action. Actions become character. Character becomes destiny.

TOPIC OF MEETING	DAY / DATE

NOTES

ACTION ITEMS	DUE

Thoughts become words. Words become action. Actions become character. Character becomes destiny.

TOPIC OF MEETING	DAY / DATE

NOTES

ACTION ITEMS	DUE

Thoughts become words. Words become action. Actions become character. Character becomes destiny.

TOPIC OF MEETING	DAY / DATE

NOTES

ACTION ITEMS	DUE

Thoughts become words. Words become action. Actions become character. Character becomes destiny.

TOPIC OF MEETING	DAY / DATE

NOTES

ACTION ITEMS	DUE

Thoughts become words. Words become action. Actions become character. Character becomes destiny.

TOPIC OF MEETING	DAY / DATE

NOTES

ACTION ITEMS	DUE

Thoughts become words. Words become action. Actions become character. Character becomes destiny.

TOPIC OF MEETING	DAY / DATE

NOTES

ACTION ITEMS	DUE

Thoughts become words. Words become action. Actions become character. Character becomes destiny.

TOPIC OF MEETING	DAY / DATE

NOTES

ACTION ITEMS	DUE

Thoughts become words. Words become action. Actions become character. Character becomes destiny.

TOPIC OF MEETING	DAY / DATE

NOTES

ACTION ITEMS	DUE

Thoughts become words. Words become action. Actions become character. Character becomes destiny.

TOPIC OF MEETING	DAY / DATE

NOTES

ACTION ITEMS	DUE

Thoughts become words. Words become action. Actions become character. Character becomes destiny.

TOPIC OF MEETING	DAY / DATE

NOTES

ACTION ITEMS	DUE

Thoughts become words. Words become action. Actions become character. Character becomes destiny.

TOPIC OF MEETING	DAY / DATE

NOTES

ACTION ITEMS	DUE

Thoughts become words. Words become action. Actions become character. Character becomes destiny.

TOPIC OF MEETING	DAY / DATE

NOTES

ACTION ITEMS	DUE

Thoughts become words. Words become action. Actions become character. Character becomes destiny.

TOPIC OF MEETING	DAY / DATE

NOTES

ACTION ITEMS	DUE

Thoughts become words. Words become action. Actions become character. Character becomes destiny.

TOPIC OF MEETING	DAY / DATE

NOTES

ACTION ITEMS	DUE

Thoughts become words. Words become action. Actions become character. Character becomes destiny.

TOPIC OF MEETING	DAY / DATE

NOTES

ACTION ITEMS	DUE

Thoughts become words. Words become action. Actions become character. Character becomes destiny.

TOPIC OF MEETING	DAY / DATE

NOTES

ACTION ITEMS	DUE

Thoughts become words. Words become action. Actions become character. Character becomes destiny.

TOPIC OF MEETING	DAY / DATE

NOTES

ACTION ITEMS	DUE

Thoughts become words. Words become action. Actions become character. Character becomes destiny.

TOPIC OF MEETING	DAY / DATE

NOTES

ACTION ITEMS	DUE

Thoughts become words. Words become action. Actions become character. Character becomes destiny.

TOPIC OF MEETING	DAY / DATE

NOTES

ACTION ITEMS	DUE

Thoughts become words. Words become action. Actions become character. Character becomes destiny.

TOPIC OF MEETING	DAY / DATE

NOTES

ACTION ITEMS	DUE

Thoughts become words. Words become action. Actions become character. Character becomes destiny.

TOPIC OF MEETING	DAY / DATE

NOTES

ACTION ITEMS	DUE

Thoughts become words. Words become action. Actions become character. Character becomes destiny.

TOPIC OF MEETING	DAY / DATE

NOTES

ACTION ITEMS	DUE

Thoughts become words. Words become action. Actions become character. Character becomes destiny.

TOPIC OF MEETING	DAY / DATE

NOTES

ACTION ITEMS	DUE

Thoughts become words. Words become action. Actions become character. Character becomes destiny.

TOPIC OF MEETING	DAY / DATE

NOTES

ACTION ITEMS	DUE

Thoughts become words. Words become action. Actions become character. Character becomes destiny.

TOPIC OF MEETING	DAY / DATE

NOTES

ACTION ITEMS	DUE

Thoughts become words. Words become action. Actions become character. Character becomes destiny.

TOPIC OF MEETING	DAY / DATE

NOTES

ACTION ITEMS	DUE

Thoughts become words. Words become action. Actions become character. Character becomes destiny.

TOPIC OF MEETING	DAY / DATE

NOTES

ACTION ITEMS	DUE

Thoughts become words. Words become action. Actions become character. Character becomes destiny.

TOPIC OF MEETING	DAY / DATE

NOTES

ACTION ITEMS	DUE

Thoughts become words. Words become action. Actions become character. Character becomes destiny.

Thoughts become words. Words become action. Actions become character. Character becomes destiny.